ROMAN BRITAIN

Fiona Macdonald

Series editor Sue Palmer

OXFORD
UNIVERSITY PRESS

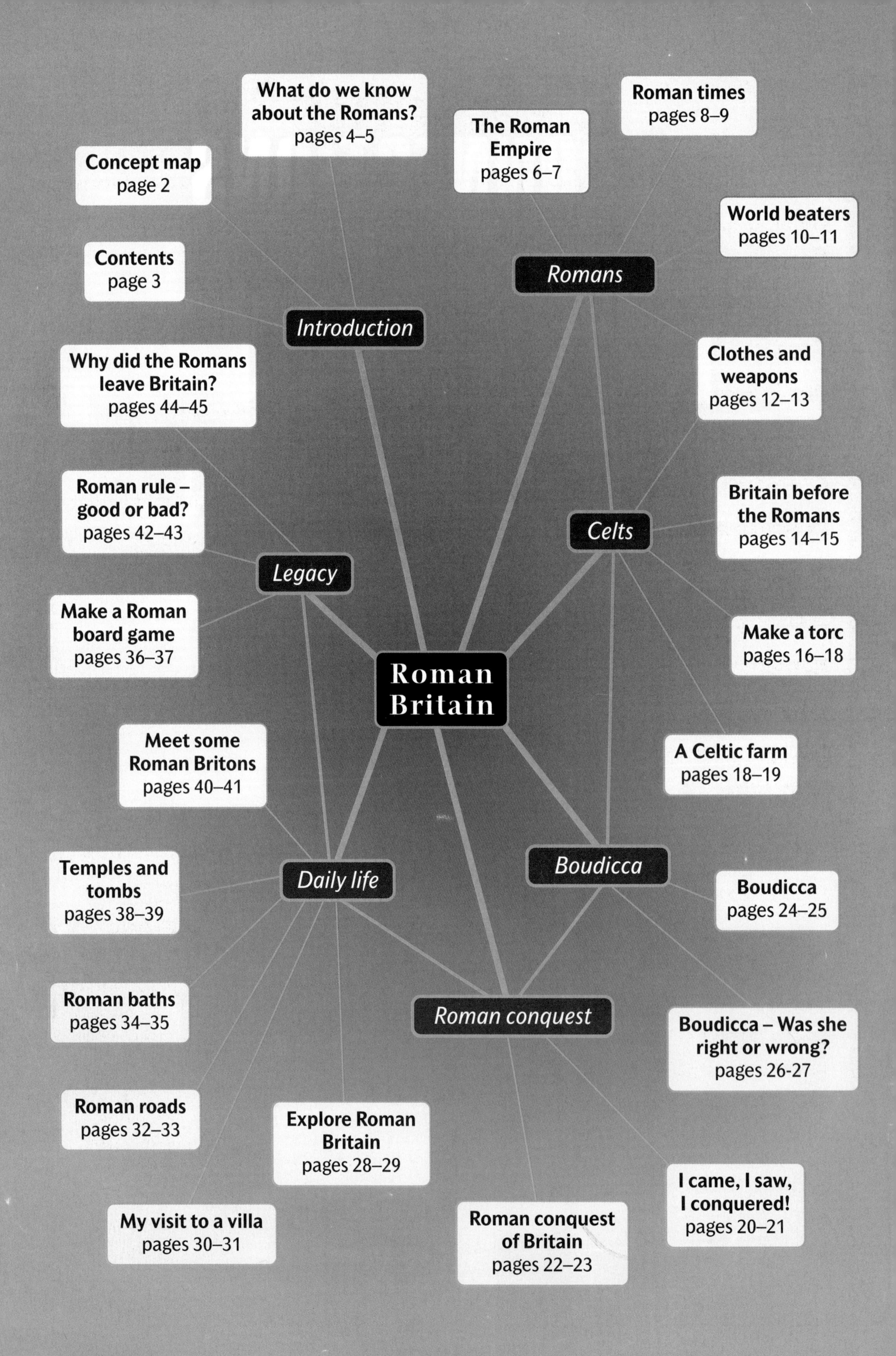

Roman Britain
Introduction
Concept map
page 2
Contents
page 3
What do we know about the Romans?
pages 4–5
Romans
The Roman Empire
pages 6–7
Roman times
pages 8–9
World beaters
pages 10–11
Clothes and weapons
pages 12–13
Celts
Britain before the Romans
pages 14–15
Make a torc
pages 16–18
A Celtic farm
pages 18–19
Roman conquest
I came, I saw, I conquered!
pages 20–21
Roman conquest of Britain
pages 22–23
Boudicca
Boudicca
pages 24–25
Boudicca – Was she right or wrong?
pages 26-27
Daily life
Explore Roman Britain
pages 28–29
My visit to a villa
pages 30–31
Roman roads
pages 32–33
Roman baths
pages 34–35
Temples and tombs
pages 38–39
Meet some Roman Britons
pages 40–41
Legacy
Make a Roman board game
pages 36–37
Roman rule – good or bad?
pages 42–43
Why did the Romans leave Britain?
pages 44–45

Contents

The Romans were brilliant at building roads and towns, and they introduced public baths and lavatories. The pages I like best are about their multiracial society, and about Boudicca. She was a great fighter, but was her revolt a good thing?

Adam Hart-Davis
BBC history programme presenter

What do we know about

The Romans lived in Italy over 2000 years ago. At first, they were farmers. But then they fought against other people in Italy, and took over their lands. This made them rich and very powerful.

The ruins of the ancient Forum, or market square, can still be seen in Rome today.

Splendid city

The Romans turned their home town, Rome, into a splendid city. It had palaces and temples, sports arenas, shopping malls, take-away food shops, schools, libraries, public baths and lavatories, and the first-ever blocks of flats. (The Romans called them 'insulae', which means 'islands', because each block was a separate community.) Rome was also the centre of a huge network of well-made roads.

Roman people

The city of Rome grew very quickly. Many different people lived there – rich nobles and businessmen, ordinary workers and slaves. By AD 300, a million people lived in Rome. It was the largest city in the world.

Huge sports arenas like the Colosseum show us how Roman people liked to spend their leisure time.

the Romans?

Roman remains

The remains of many ancient Roman buildings still survive today. They show us what life was like in Roman times. Vast underground drains, long bridges and tall **aqueducts** tell us about Roman engineering methods.

Statues and carvings, which were used to decorate important buildings, tell us what Roman people looked like. This one shows a butcher's shop.

Army and empire

The Roman army was the best in the world. Roman soldiers marched out of Italy and conquered lands in Europe, North Africa, and the Middle East. They conquered most of Britain, too. The conquered lands were called the Roman **empire**. Everyone living in the empire had to pay Roman **taxes** and obey Roman laws. To keep control, Roman soldiers lived in camps and forts all over the empire. They guarded **frontiers** and tried to stop conquered peoples rebelling against Roman rule. But after many centuries, there were more and more attacks, and the Roman empire was destroyed.

The Romans built this huge aqueduct to carry water to the city of Nimes, in France

The Roman Empire

This map shows the lands and peoples ruled by Rome around AD117. That was when the Roman empire was biggest and strongest. It measured 4000 kilometres from east to west.

THE ROMAN EMPIRE IN AD117
wine
gold
grain
lead
wool
tin
pottery
horses
glass
slaves
N
W
E
S
Black Sea
Caspian Sea
ARMENIA
CARIA
SYRIA
River Euphrates
ASIA

Roman times

The Romans were successful rulers and conquerors for nearly 1000 years.

According to legend, Rome was founded by twins Romulus and Remus who were brought up by a wolf.

1000 BC — First families settle on site of Rome, in central Italy.

509 BC — Romans get rid of kings. Rome becomes a **republic** (people choose their leaders).

334-250 BC — Roman armies conquer all Italy.

55-54 BC — Caesar attempts to conquer Britain in 55 BC and 54 BC.

30 BC — By now, Romans rule France, Spain, Greece, North Africa and Judea (modern Israel and Palestine).

27 BC — Roman republic ends. Rome now ruled by powerful men called **emperors**.

AD 43 — Romans invade Britain with 40,000 troops.

Roman ships fighting a sea battle, imagined by a 19th-century artist

Augustus, the first Roman emperor

This huge carved column still stands in Rome. It shows Trajan's soldiers fighting battles.

AD 117

Roman **empire** reaches its largest under Emperor Trajan.

AD 212

All free people living in the Roman empire given legal rights, as '**citizens**'.

AD 260

Vandals, Goths and Visigoths, warriors (from north and east), begin to attack Roman empire.

AD 395

Roman empire is divided in two – eastern part ruled from Constantinople (now Istanbul, in Turkey), western part ruled from Rome.

AD 401

Roman soldiers begin to leave Britain to go and defend city of Rome.

AD 455

City of Rome destroyed by the Vandals.

AD 476

End of empire in west.

Roman lands in the east become part of the new Byzantine empire, under the Emperor Constantine (shown right), which lasts until AD 1453.

The King of the Vandals entering Rome, imagined by a 19th-century artist.

World beaters

Why were Roman soldiers so successful?

① Reasons they became soldiers

- they thought Rome had best **empire**
- keen to fight – joined army as **volunteers**
- well paid and well fed
- got land and money when they retired

The Roman Army

an efficient, well-equipped, healthy, keen fighting force

② Strength and fitness

- all healthy, tall, and strong
- did exercises to keep them fit and make them tough

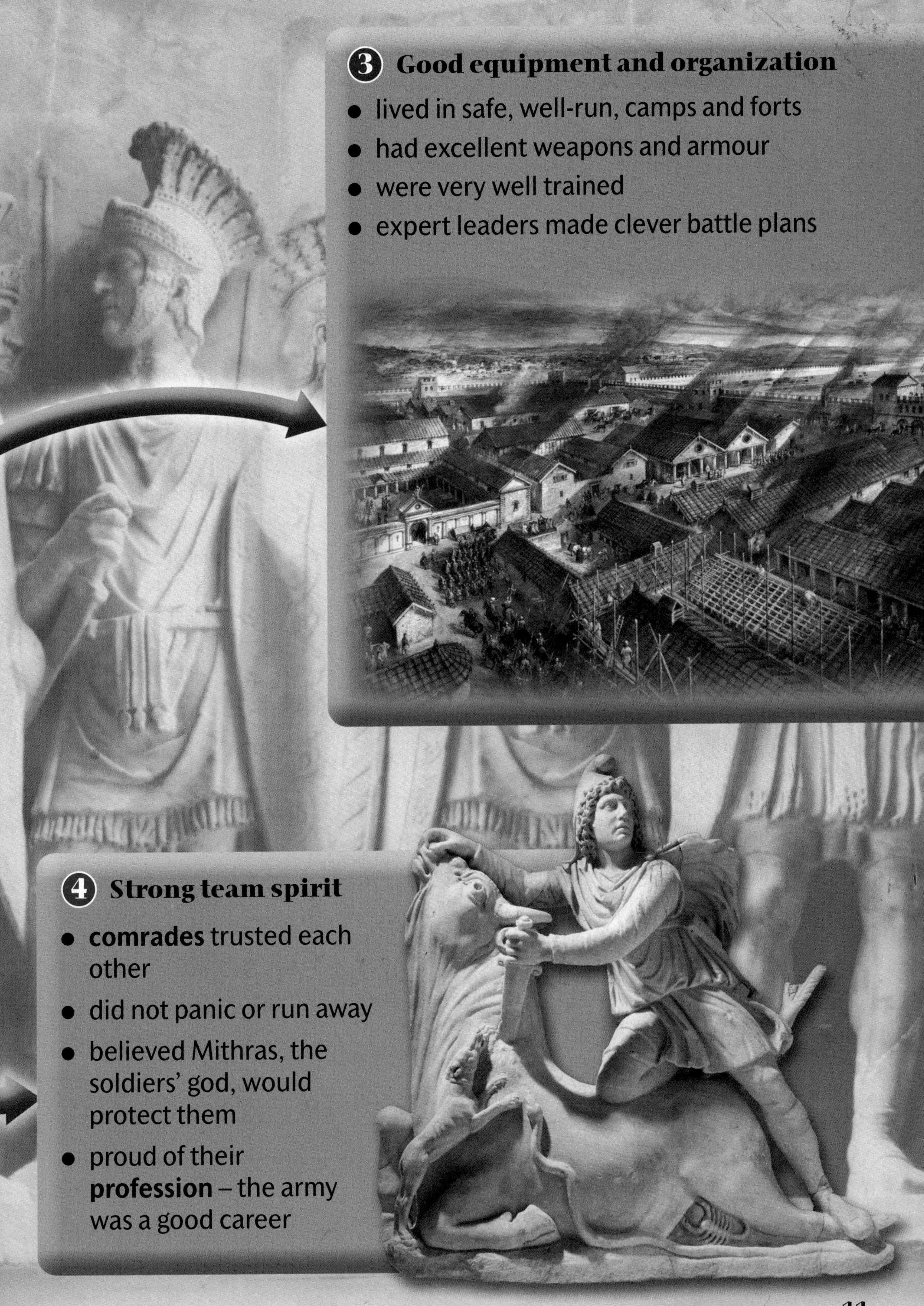

3 Good equipment and organization

- lived in safe, well-run, camps and forts
- had excellent weapons and armour
- were very well trained
- expert leaders made clever battle plans

4 Strong team spirit

- **comrades** trusted each other
- did not panic or run away
- believed Mithras, the soldiers' god, would protect them
- proud of their **profession** – the army was a good career

Clothes and weapons

Roman soldier

Appearance

- dark eyes
- suntanned skin
- always shaved

Clothes

- tunic with short sleeves (thick wool) dyed red so blood would not show
- cloak – sometimes with hood (thick, warm wool)
- underpants (wool – or linen made from flax plants) copied from Celts – useful in cold countries

Footwear

- lace-up leather sandals (or leather boots)
- leather soles were studded with nails (so they would last longer)
- socks (wool) – for cold countries like Britain

Hair

- dark
- cut short

Weapons and armour

- heavy armour (leather and metal)
- helmet
- breast-plate
- stomach protector
- strong leather belt
- scabbards (long leather pockets to carry swords and dagger)
- long sword (for slashing)
- short sword (for stabbing)
- rectangular shield (wood covered with leather), metal 'boss' in centre to protect hand
- javelin (long wooden spear)
- sharp metal tip on javelin

Roman soldiers trained by walking up to 30 km each day!

Celtic warrior

Appearance

- very tall
- strong muscles
- light-coloured eyes
- white skin (red when angry)
- long moustache
- body-paint (woad – made from plants)

Hair

- brushed back (to look like horse's mane)
- smeared with sticky lime and water (to make it stand up on end)
- red or fair hair (or dark hair bleached with lime)

Clothes

- sleeveless tunic (wool or linen)
- striped woollen cloak (coloured with plant dyes)
- checked woollen trousers (coloured with plant dyes)
- leather belt

Jewellery

- **torc** (bronze or silver)
- brooch (silver and enamel – coloured glass)

Weapons and armour

- round shield made from wood or metal
- sword with iron blade
- spear (wooden handle, iron tip)

Footwear

- leather boots

A Celtic warrior had to pay a fine if he got so fat that his belt no longer fitted.

Britain before the Romans

The Celts

The Celts lived in Britain before the Romans invaded. Celtic chieftains were in power between 1000–100 BC.

They overpowered the people who lived there before.

The Celts in Britain were divided into many different **tribes**, for example, the Brigantes, who lived in Yorkshire, and the Silures, who lived in South Wales. Celtic tribes also lived in Spain, northern Italy, Belgium, Switzerland, Austria and France. They traded valuable goods with each other, such as weapons and pottery. Sometimes they fought.

This map shows where Celtic tribes lived in Britain.

Celtic culture

All Celtic peoples shared a similar way of life, speaking Celtic languages, making Celtic-style art and music, and worshipping Celtic gods. Celtic culture was very different from Roman culture. That was one reason why the Romans and Celts often quarrelled.

A living from the land

Most Celtic families were farmers. They grew wheat and oats to make bread and porridge. They kept cattle and sheep to provide meat, milk and wool. They gathered wild foods, and hunted wild animals.

Useful crafts

Celtic farmers and craftworkers made all kinds of useful things by hand. They had no big machines to help them. They made farm tools and weapons from iron. They wove warm woollen cloth with fancy check patterns. They made pottery decorated with swirling designs.

A Celtic pottery bowl

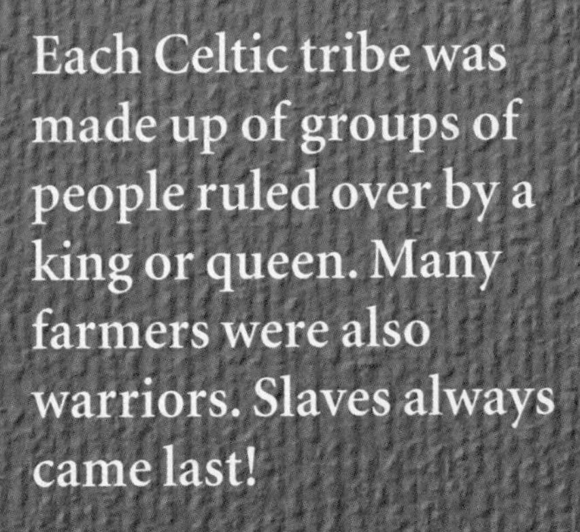

Each Celtic tribe was made up of groups of people ruled over by a king or queen. Many farmers were also warriors. Slaves always came last!

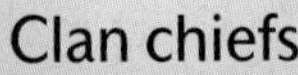

Farmers and Warriors

Slaves

How to make a torc

Torcs were heavy rings, made of gold, silver or other valuable metals. Celtic people wore them round their necks. The Celts believed torcs had magic powers to protect them from harm. Celtic warriors sometimes fought wearing torcs and body-paint – but nothing else!

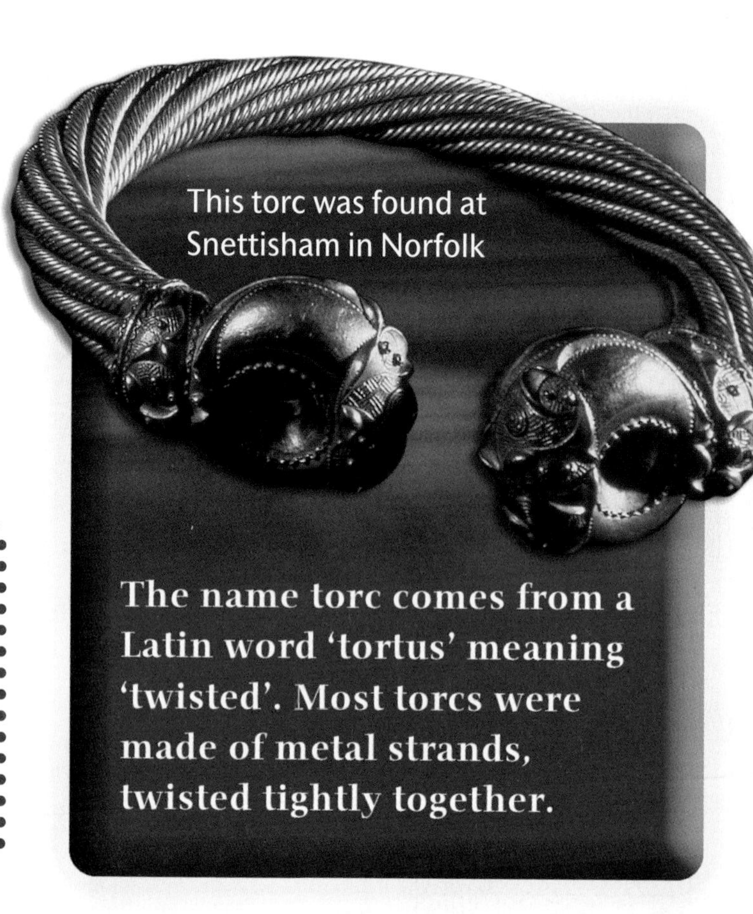

This torc was found at Snettisham in Norfolk

The name torc comes from a Latin word 'tortus' meaning 'twisted'. Most torcs were made of metal strands, twisted tightly together.

You will need:

- tape measure
- pencil and paper
- modelling clay
- modelling tool
- gold or silver paint
- paintbrush

1. Measure the distance round your neck, very loosely. Write down the measurement.
2. Roll out two or three strands of modelling clay (about 10 cm longer than your neck measurement).
3. Twist the strands together carefully.
4. Shape each end of the twisted strands into a loop, a disc or a ball.
5. Add patterns using the modelling tool.
6. Arrange your torc in a curved shape. Do not bring the ends too close together, or you will not be able to put it on.
7. Wait for it to harden.
8. Paint your torc gold or silver, and leave in a warm place to dry.

Celtic patterns

Roman writers reported that the Celts painted their faces and bodies before going into battle. They used woad (a blue dye, made from plants). They believed that the painted patterns would protect them from harm.

Pottery and metal work

We know that the Celts were very skilled craftworkers because many examples of their beautiful jewellery, pottery, weapons and armour have been found at burial sites.

▲
The famous 'Battersea Shield', found in the River Thames, can be seen with other Celtic treasures in the British Museum.

▲
A pottery vase found in the barrow (burial chamber) at Kernevez in France.

A bronze disc from the Celtic cart burial in France. ▶

A Celtic farm
This picture of a Celtic farm shows how the farmhouse was built and how the farmer's family lived and worked.
smoke drifting up through the thatch
meat (preserved by smoke from fire)
hay-rick
cattle (for meat, milk, butter and cheese)
thatch (bundles of straw)
goats (for milk and meat)
farm tools and weapons hung on pegs fixed to walls
storage pit, for grain
sheep's fleece
weaving cloth on a loom
woollen blankets
horse's head (or enemy's head!) for good luck
pottery jars (for storage)
iron cooking pot
open fire
oven for baking bread
hearth
wooden poles
earth floor
spinning
wattle and daub walls made from woven twigs plastered with mud, clay and chalk
stone weight
sledge (dragged by oxen)
bed of dry bracken or straw
quern (two stones, used to grind wheat grains into flour)
wooden bucket

KEY
Building materials
Heating and cooking
Working at home
Farm animals
Farm tools
Wild foods
sheep (for meat and wool)
wild boar
plough
pigs (for meat and bristles)
wild fish (from stream)
animal skins
wild deer
metal-tipped plough
sieve for soil
spade
pitchfork
sickle (for cutting corn)
wild berries, mushrooms, nuts (from forests)
pottery jar
baskets woven from twigs and grass

I came, I saw, I conquere

The life of Julius Caesar

What was Caesar like?

Julius Caesar was one of the most extraordinary men who ever lived. He was tough, brave, proud, boastful, and very ambitious. He was clever and cunning, and had amazing energy.

This stone carving, made in ancient Roman times, shows us what Caesar looked like. Roman people thought he was good-looking, but said he was vain!

Caesar's early life

Caesar was born in 100 BC. He came from an ancient noble family in Rome. When he was 21, he joined the army for six years (81-75 BC), to train to be a soldier. Then he decided to leave the army. On his way home to Rome, Caesar was captured by pirates.

Roman ships had many oars and a large sail.

He threatened to kill the pirates, if ever he got free. He managed to escape, then hunted and caught them, and arranged for them to be killed in a very horrible way. After this, Caesar worked as a **lawyer** in Rome for the next 12 years, and also became a **politician**.

Caesar was famous for his wit. He wrote a joke book but, sadly, it has not survived.

His army career

In 61 BC, the Roman **government** asked Caesar to become an army commander in Spain. He defeated other dangerous enemies, including British King Cassivellaunus. He organized the first and second Roman invasions of Britain, in 55 BC and again in 54 BC, but the Romans did not stay for long. Caesar led his soldiers to win many victories, especially in Gaul (France), which he conquered in 51 BC.

Ruler of Rome

Caesar's victories made him very famous and very popular. The Romans asked him to be 'dictator' (strong-man and ruler) of their **empire** – for life! He made many new laws, and reorganized the Roman calendar. The month of July is still named after him.

While fighting in North Africa, Caesar fell in love with the famous and beautiful Queen Cleopatra of Egypt, although he already had a wife and family in Rome.

Caesar was also famous for his short, snappy sayings. He reported on one battle he fought in just three words: 'Veni, Vidi, Vici!' (*'I came, I saw, I conquered!'*)

Caesar's enemies

Caesar said that everything he did was meant to help Rome. This was probably true. But some people in Rome did not believe him. They said he wanted power and glory for himself. So they murdered him in 44 BC.

The death of Julius Caesar, imagined by a 19th-century artist.

Roman conquest of

The Romans first invaded Britain in 55 BC, led by Julius Caesar, but they soon left. About 90 years later, they returned again – this time to stay!

How the Romans took control of Britain

AD 41

Claudius becomes **emperor** of Rome.

AD 43

Claudius sends 40,000 troops to invade Britain – they land in Kent.

Troops march inland. Celts are defeated.

Romans capture Colchester.

AD 47

Romans defeat Celtic King Caratacus, leader of the Catuvellauni **tribe**.

Caratacus escapes. Seeks shelter with Celtic Brigantes tribe.

AD 49

Romans build new settlement at Colchester.

AD 51

Celtic Queen Cartimandua of the Brigantes is friendly with Romans – **betrays** Caratacus.

AD 61

Celtic Queen Boudicca leads rebellion against Rome.

Britain

Roman governor Cerealis starts new Roman conquests in northern England.

AD 71

Roman governor Agricola conquers lands in Wales and along Scottish border. Agricola fights Scottish highland warriors.

AD 84

Romans build Antonine Wall in Scotland, north of Hadrian's Wall. But they cannot defend it, and leave it in AD 160.

AD 140

AD 73-77

Roman governor Frontinus conquers Celtic tribes in Wales.

AD 122

Peak of Roman power in Britain. Romans begin to build Hadrian's Wall, to defend land and people south of Scottish border.

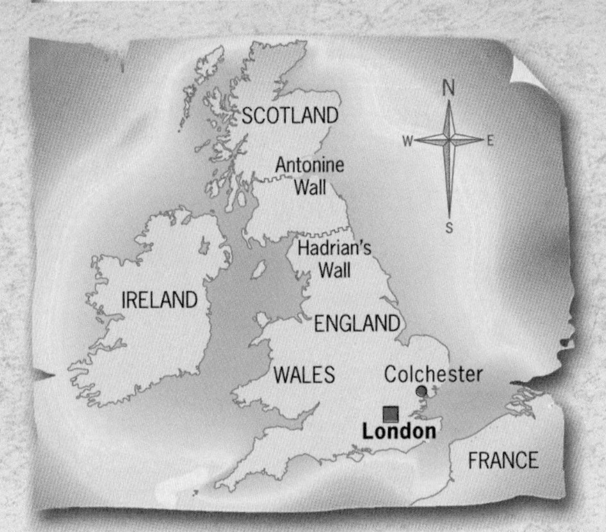

Boudicca

AD 43-60

When Roman invaders landed in Britain the Celtic people of the Iceni **tribe** welcomed them. They asked the Roman soldiers to protect them from other Celts who were their enemies.

But when the the king of the Iceni died, his wife, Queen Boudicca, decided to rule alone without Roman help. The Iceni people feared that this might make the Romans angry. They were right!

Later in AD 61

AD 61 at the same time ...

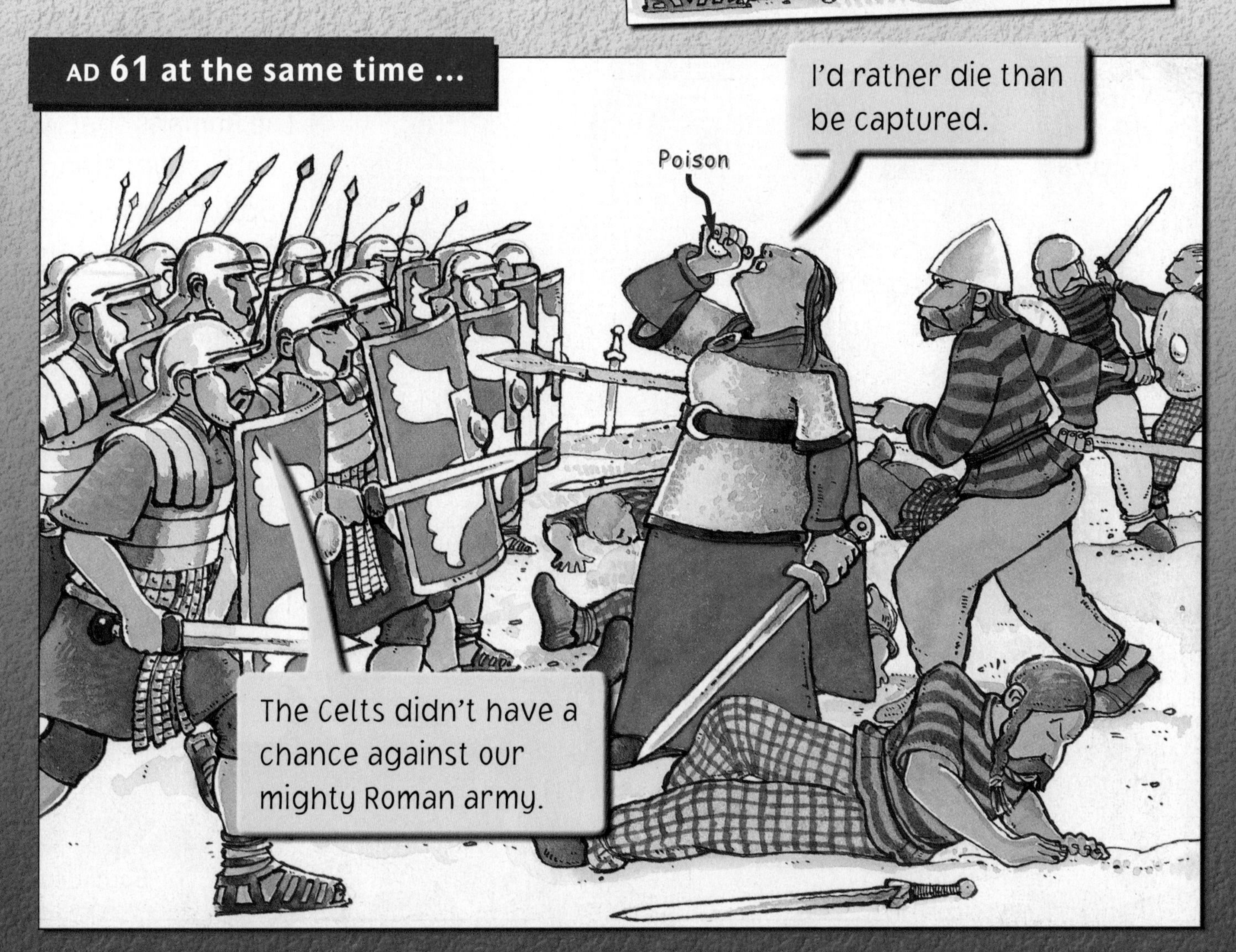

Boudicca - Was she right

Over 70,000 Roman and Celtic people were killed during Boudicca's rebellion, and thousands of homes were destroyed. Was she right to rebel, and cause so much suffering?

or wrong?

citizens of Colchester

Boudicca wrecked our city and killed our families!

She used to be our friend! She's a **traitor** to Rome!

Roman governor

I'm glad Boudicca rebelled. It gave us an excuse to conquer her kingdom.

Roman Emperor Nero

Roman soldier

Anyone who attacks the Romans deserves to die!

Explore Roman Britain

Welcome to Roman Britain – come and explore all the main attractions!

Aquae Sulis (Bath)

Tired and dirty after the long journey from Rome?

Why not visit Aquae Sulis – a holy city – and relax in the warm waters of the best Roman baths in Brittania?

You can drink the hot spring waters to cure any sickness, then give thanks at the Temple of Minerva before you travel on your way.

Camulodunum (Colchester)

- first Roman base in Britain
- retired Roman soldiers live here
- magnificent temple and huge entrance gate

Castra (Chester)

- largest Roman arena in Britain (8000 seats)
- see gladiators fight here

Euburacum (York)

- two great army forts built here as well as walled town

Isca (Caerleon)

- largest army fort in Wales
- holds 6000 soldiers

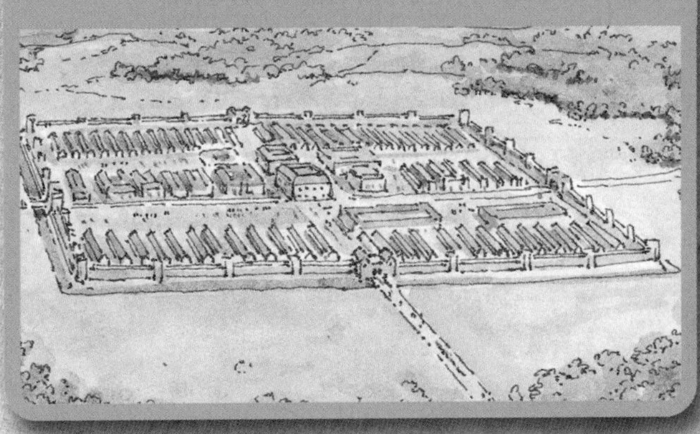

Fishbourne Roman Villa

- biggest and best Roman villa in Britain
- painted walls, marble statues and lovely gardens
- fine **mosaic** floors

Londinium (London)

- biggest city in Britain
- great centre of trade
- ships arrive carrying soldiers – take away British goods, to sell overseas

Hadrian's Wall

- huge stone barrier nearly 120 km long
- 16 forts built along it
- guards Roman empire from attack by fierce **tribes** further north

Verulanium (St Albans)

- home of St Alban (Roman soldier who became a Christian – executed for refusing to give up his faith)
- beautiful open-air theatre

My visit to a villa

Villas were huge houses in the country. They belonged to rich, powerful Romans. Celtic kings and queens who were friendly with the Romans sometimes sent their sons to live in Roman villas, so they would find out about Roman customs, and learn to speak Latin.

A Roman Villa
Fishbourne
Sussex

Dear Mum and Dad

I got to the villa yesterday. The journey took two whole days. When we arrived, all dirty, a bossy slave made me go to the bath-house. There was a room full of steam, where the slave wiped all the mud off me, and a huge pool of warm water to swim in. Then I met the other two boys who are Celtic princes like me. We've got to learn about Roman ways, and how to speak Latin.

The villa is enormous. It has sixty different rooms! It's made of stone, and there are huge pillars – as big as tree-trunks – holding up the roof. Inside, the floors are covered with pictures, made of tiny bits of coloured clay. The walls are painted with pictures, too and there are stone statues everywhere – they remind me of ghosts. There's a garden, with a fountain, right in the middle of the villa!

After exploring the house, we went outside. They have rooms for horses, called 'stables', cattle-sheds, barns full of grain and hay, and big brick buildings where the slaves sleep. They have fruit trees in the garden – the Romans don't pick wild fruit, like us – and lots of herbs and vegetables, growing in neat rows. We noticed plants with strange purple and orange roots which the Romans brought from Italy. I think they are called carrots. Do you think they will be safe to eat?

At dinner, there were funny wooden things to sit on, called chairs, and beds on legs, called couches. The grown-up Romans lay down on them to eat their meals. The food was cooked in a separate room called a kitchen. After dark, they set fire to oil in little pots to make the room bright. And I noticed another strange thing – all the floors felt hot!

The teacher has called us to our lessons, so I must go now.

Your loving son
Caratacus (prince)

A fountain in the courtyard of a villa.

A dining room in a Roman villa would have looked like this museum model.

Roman roads

The Romans were great **engineers**. Roman inventions included cranes, concrete **aqueducts**, floating bridges, underground drains and sewers, piped water supplies, public lavatories, domed roofs, and very well-made roads. Romans made their roads as straight as possible, avoiding steep hills and marshy valleys. So the first job was to plan a good route ......

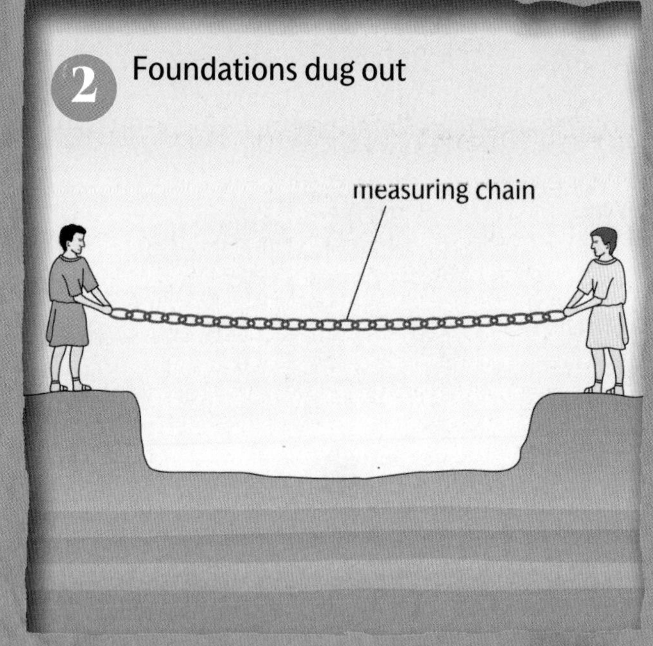

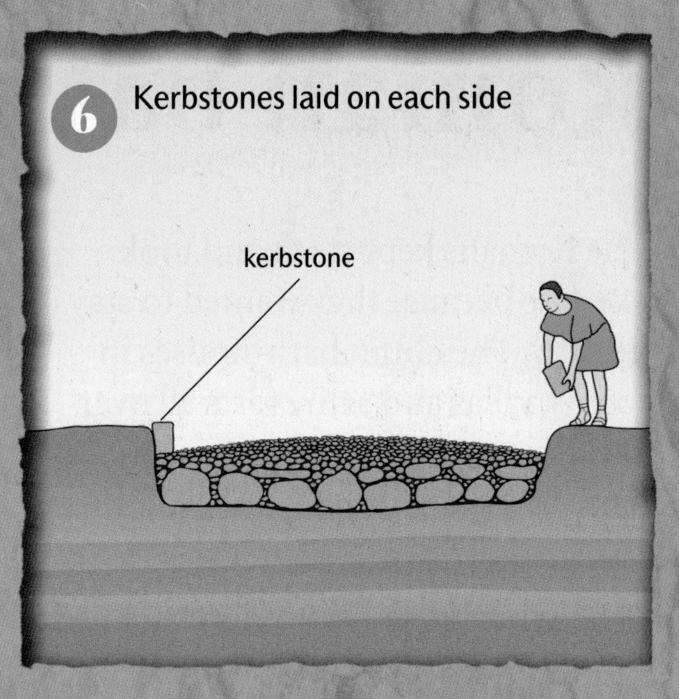

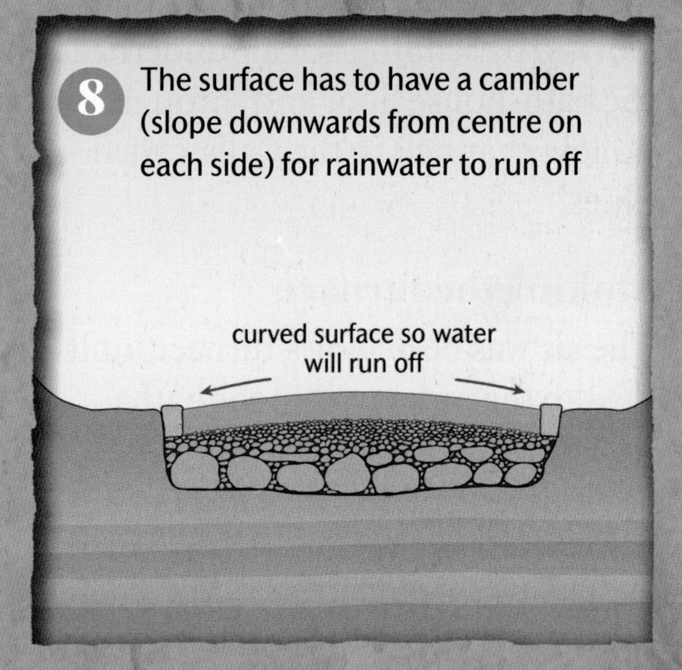

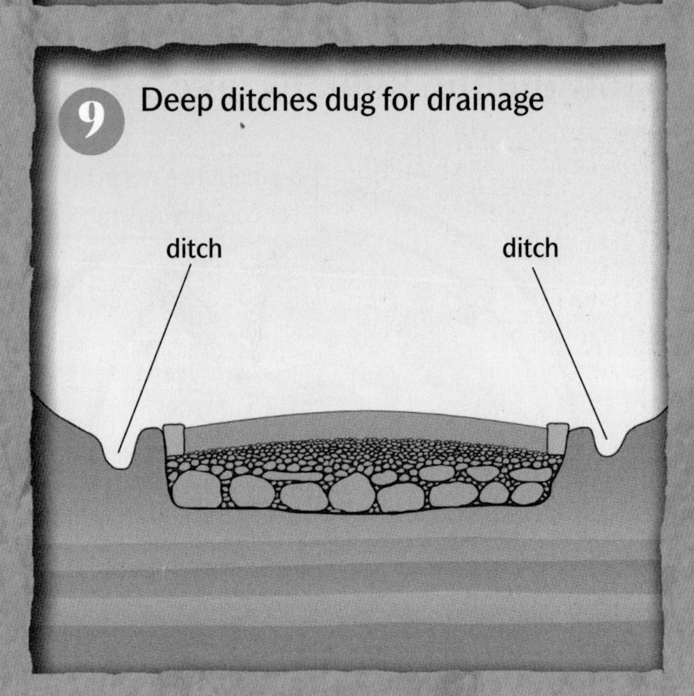

Milestones were placed beside the road to mark each mile from London. A Roman mile = 1480 metres (1.48 km).

The Romans built 85,300 km of roads in their empire.

mile post

Roman baths

The Romans kept clean and took exercise because they wanted to stay healthy. They built bath-houses in towns, villas and army forts all over Britain, often with sports centres close by.

How were Roman baths heated?

Roman bath-houses were heated by an invention called a hypocaust. This worked by sending hot air underneath the bath-house floor and through hollow channels in the walls, called 'flues'.

Stoking the furnace

The air was heated by a furnace built next to the outer wall of the bath-house. Slaves kept the furnace-fires burning. In Britain, they used brushwood as fuel.

Through the hypocaust

As the fire burned, the draught created by the flues 'pulled' the hot air from the furnace under the bath-house floors and up through the walls. Then it escaped outside along with smoke from the burning wood.

Steam cleaning

As the hot air flowed through the hypocaust, it gave up some of its heat, and the bath-house floor became hot. The bathers splashed water onto the hot floor to make the steam that helped them sweat and get clean.

Cooling off

The rooms next to the furnace were the hottest, because the air flowing under their floors was full of heat from the fire. The rooms further away from the furnace were cooler because the air from the furnace had lost a lot of its heat by the time it reached their floors.

The pool

The pool in the hot room was filled with warm water from a tank set into the floor. The bottom of the tank was heated from underneath by hot air, just like the bath-house floor. When the water in the tank became warm, it rose to the top of the pool. When the water in the pool cooled, it dropped to the bottom of the tank. There, it was quickly heated up again.

How did the Romans take a bath?

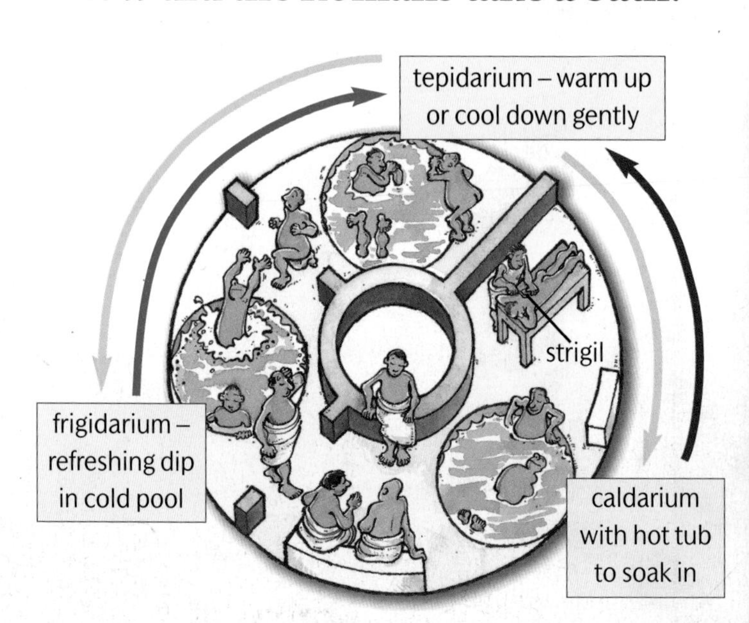

The public baths

Central heating

Hypocausts were also used to provide central heating in rich Romans' houses. The hot air from a furnace flowed under all the floors, making them feel warm.

Make a Roman board

Roman soldiers often played dice or board games to pass the time. This board game has been played for thousands of years. Roman soldiers scratched the pattern on stone to play it when they were off duty or relaxing at the baths.

You will need:

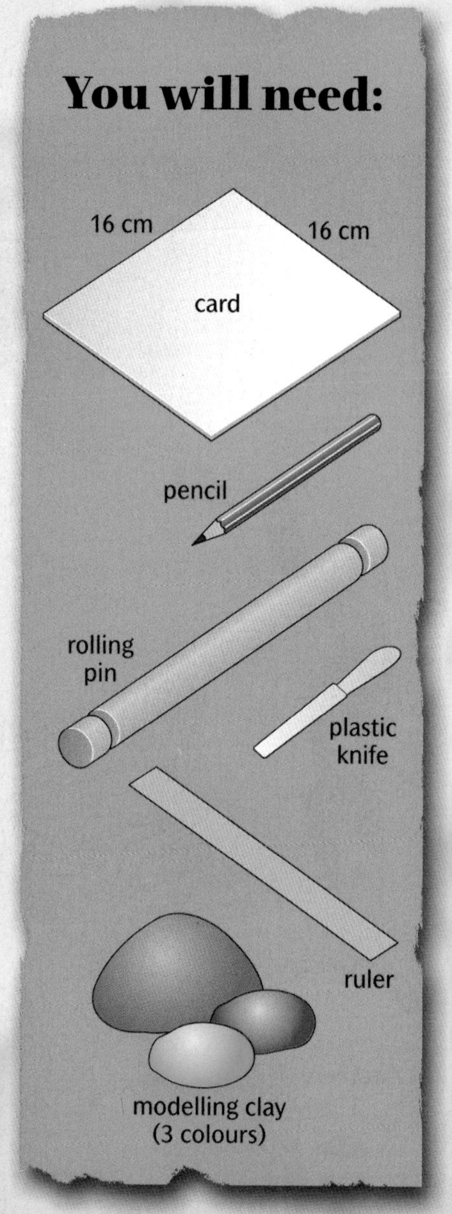

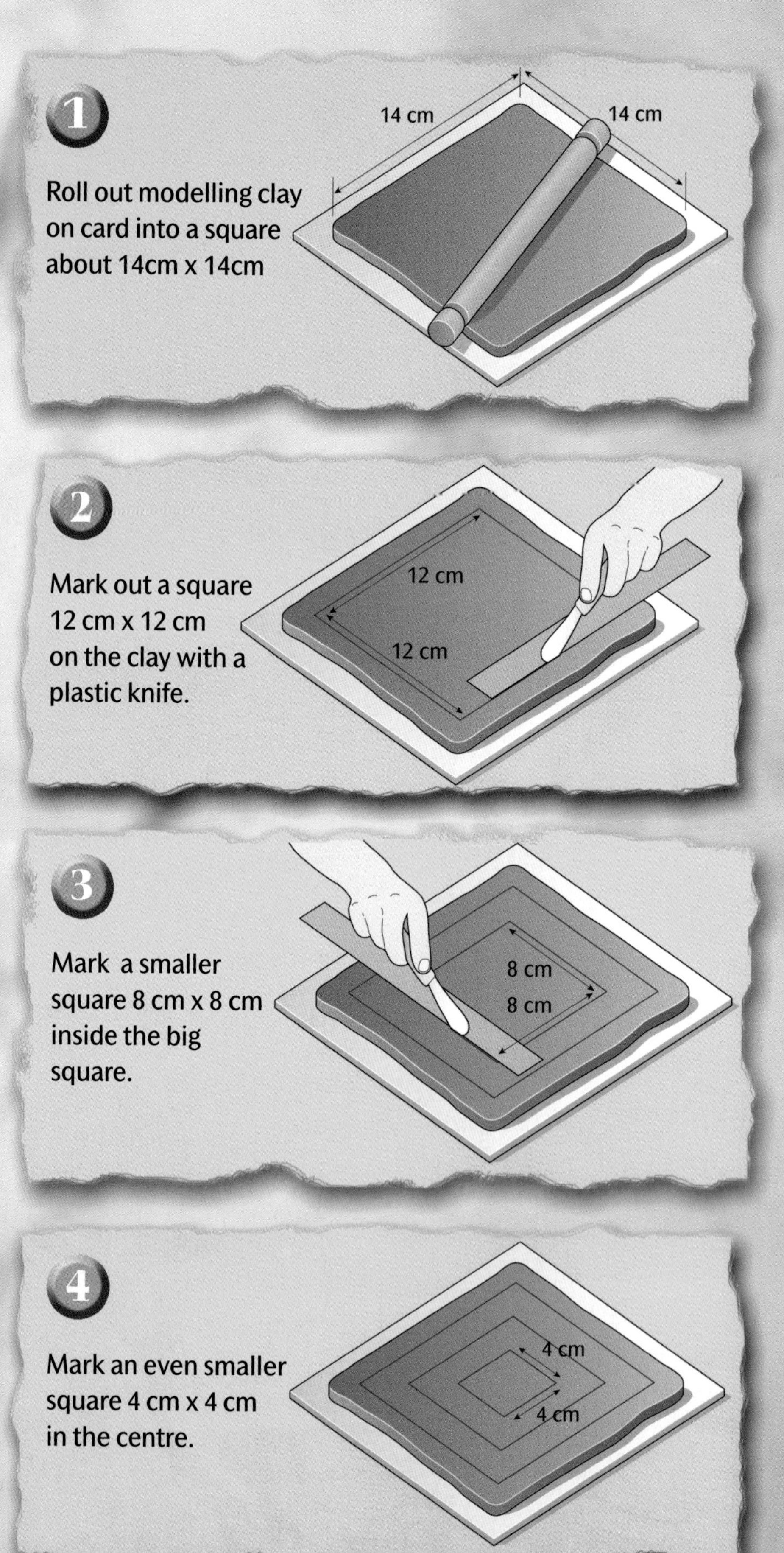

1 Roll out modelling clay on card into a square about 14cm x 14cm

2 Mark out a square 12 cm x 12 cm on the clay with a plastic knife.

3 Mark a smaller square 8 cm x 8 cm inside the big square.

4 Mark an even smaller square 4 cm x 4 cm in the centre.

game

5

Mark the centre-point of each line, and the corners, with the end of a pencil (not too deep).

6

Mark four lines, joining each set of centre points.

7

Make nine little balls in each colour from modelling clay.

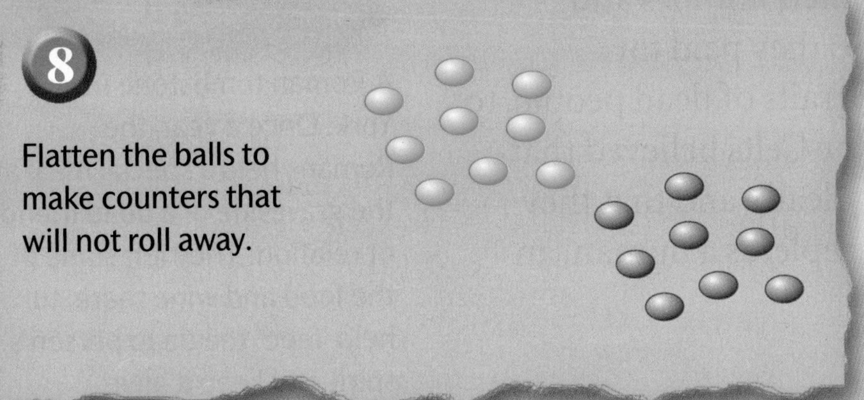

8

Flatten the balls to make counters that will not roll away.

To play

- Each player has nine counters the same colour.
- Choose a colour.
- The aim of the game is to get three of your counters in a row.
- Take turns to put a counter on a spot.

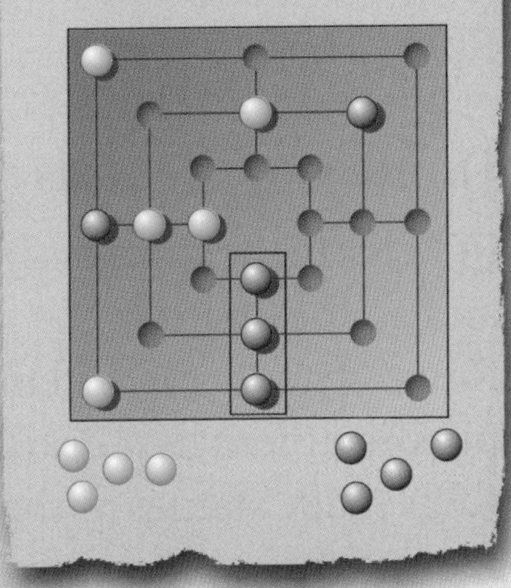

Today, some people call this game Nine Men's Morris.

Temples and tombs

A model of a temple at Vindolanda

At home in Rome, the Romans worshipped many different gods and goddesses. Jupiter was the most important. He protected the Roman state.

Celtic people also honoured many gods, such as Lug, god of music, and Epona, goddess of horses. They said prayers and gave offerings to holy mountains, rivers and trees. When the Romans came to Britain, they started to worship Celtic gods and goddesses, as well as their own. Sometimes, they joined Roman and Celtic gods together, or gave Celtic gods Roman names.

Homes for the gods

In Britain, the Romans built huge temples for gods and goddesses to live in, just like those they built in Rome. They carved lifelike statues of gods, and pictured them in **mosaics** and wall-paintings. The Celts made statues of their gods, too. They preferred to worship in the open air.

A Roman tombstone from York. Once a year, the Romans held a special meal at the graveside of a dead friend or relation. They left some of the food and wine there, to help 'feed' the dead person's spirit and keep it alive.

Remembering the dead

The Romans believed that the spirits of dead people went on living for as long as their families and friends remembered them. So they paid for tombstones, with carved portraits of dead people, to stand close to their graves. The Celts believed that people's spirits lived on after death, and that they might be born again, for example, as a human, an animal or a bird.

Pan, the Roman god of the countryside

A Celtic goddess – from a panel on a silver bowl made by Celtic craftworkers

Curses

The Romans and Celts often asked their gods to help them – or to harm their enemies! They wrote down 'curses' on scraps of lead and left them at temples.

"I curse Tretia Maria and her life and mind and memory and liver and lungs mixed up together, and her words, thoughts and memory...."

"May my silver ring be returned, and may the thief and his helpers be cursed in his blood and eyes and every limb, or even have all his intestines eaten away ...."

The 'Bath Curse' – found scratched on a piece of lead

Meet some Roman Britons

Roman Britain was a **multi-cultural** society. You could meet many different people there. Some were born in Britain. Some, such as Roman tax-collectors, came to work there for a short time. Others, such as retired Roman soldiers, settled there. A few, such as merchants and sea-captains, visited Britain regularly, on business trips.

Barates, merchant, from Syria, and his wife Regina, from Celtic Catuvellauni tribe.
Home: South Shields

All these different people lived peacefully together. Often, they were friends, and sometimes they married. Many ordinary Roman soldiers married British women. But Roman governors and army officers usually brought their wives and children with them to Britain, as well as their favourite slaves.

Flavius Verecundus, Centurion, from Hungary, and his wife, Vibia Pacata, from Africa
Home: south Scotland

A new lifestyle

In Britain, Romans and Celts did not live side-by-side. The Romans lived in towns, or army **barracks**.

The Celts lived on farms in the countryside, or in villages built outside the walls of Roman towns and forts. But Romans and Celts often met each other. Roman officials and Celtic kings discussed politics.

Rich Roman and Celtic families invited each other to their comfortable homes. Roman soldiers and slaves, and

Volusia Faustina, from Rome, and her husband Aurelius Senecio, **government** official, from Rome
Home: Lincoln

Titus, Roman soldier, from Yugoslavia, and Aurelia Aia, his daughter, born in Britain. Home: Cumbria

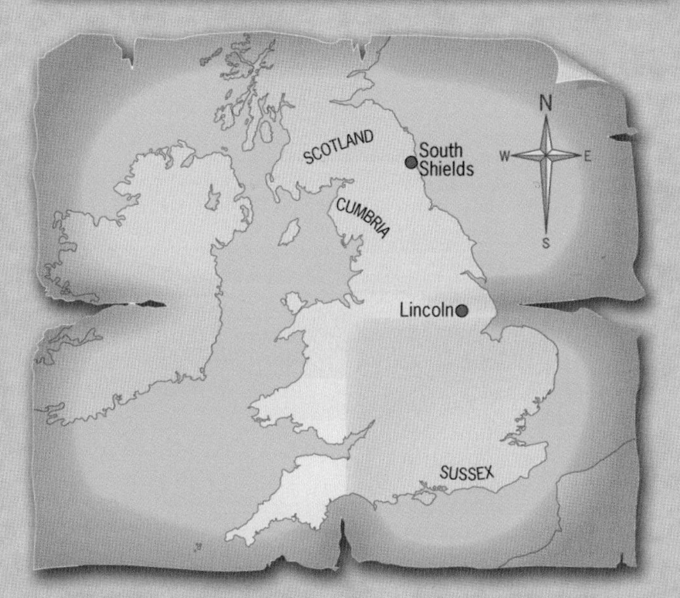

Victor, freed slave, from North Africa
Home: South Shields

Cogidubnus, Celtic King
(Regni and Arebates **tribes**)
Home: Sussex

Celtic farmers, craftworkers, cooks, horse-breeders, inn-keepers, and market-traders, worked together every day – and relaxed in bars and taverns every evening. Over the years, a new way of life developed, mixing Roman and Celtic customs, laws, ideas, beliefs and words.

Some Roman words

The Romans spoke a language called Latin. It was named after Latium, the district close to Rome where they lived. Roman soldiers and government officials spoke Latin wherever they went. So, in Britain and all over the Roman empire, the people they met and worked with had to learn how to speak Latin, too.

Today, people living in lands the Romans ruled still speak languages based on Latin. These include Italian, Spanish and French. English also contains many Latin words, and many Celtic and Saxon ones.

Some words we use that come straight from Latin

Latin	English	Latin	English
animal	animal	fungus	fungus
anchora	anchor	infans	infant
candela	candle	pirata	pirate
fragilis	fragile	poeta	poet

Roman rule – good

" We civilized them! Those Celts were just savages until we came along. No baths, no piped water, no lavatories, no sewers! No olive oil to clean their hair and skin! No soft silk robes – just itchy wool and scratchy flax. Bare feet most of the time, as well, not good leather sandals.

We taught them Latin, and how to read and write. We showed them how to use coins, for buying and selling. And we showed them how to build roads and houses properly – in brick, concrete and stone – and put in central heating.

Their farming was not well organized, either. True, they grew good crops, but we showed them how to grow more – and how to sell them in markets in cities and towns. We set up well-run mines to produce gold, silver, copper, iron and coal to sell, as well as timber. All they had thought of selling was tin.

But, let's face it, Britain is cold, wet, miserable and muddy, compared with Rome. Really, the Britons should be grateful that we came here at all."

A Roman soldier

A Roman villa

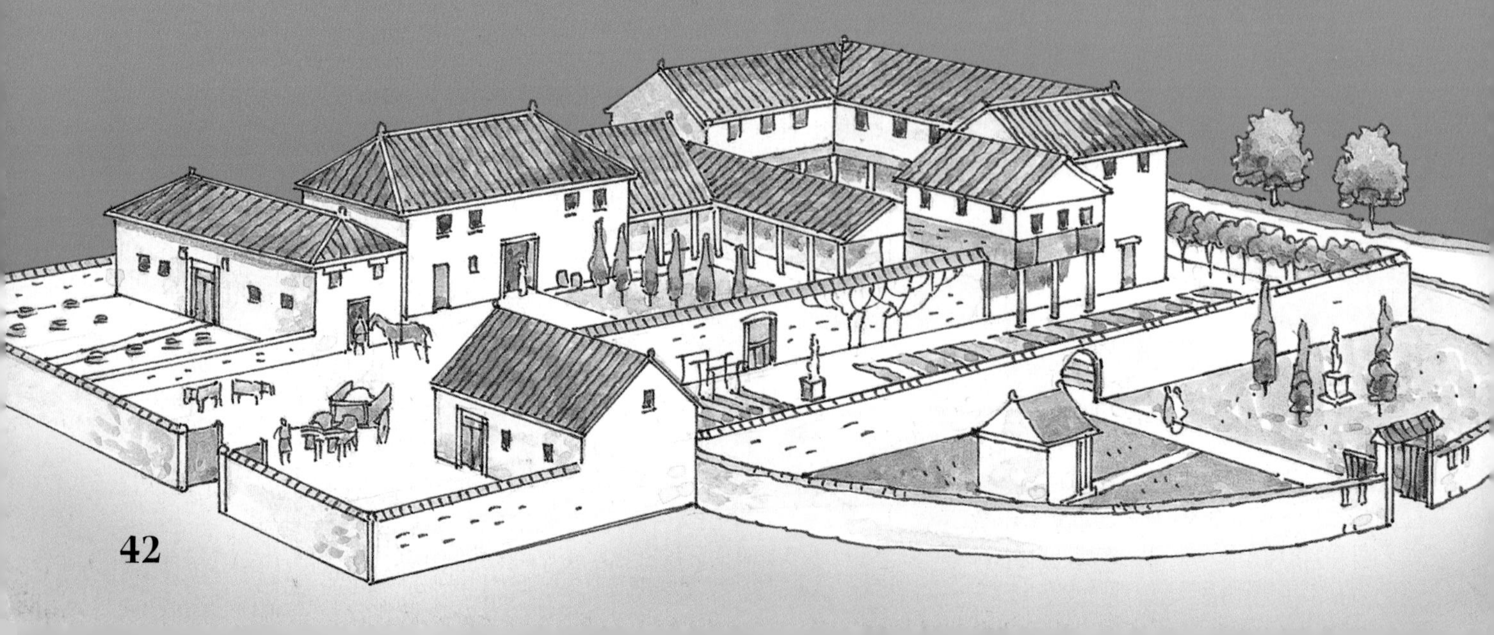

or bad?

" Just listen to him! A typical Roman. Convinced he's the best, and can't understand anything that's different. The Romans sneered at our soldiers – but they knew we were braver than them. We weren't paid to fight, like they were! We fought because we loved our chieftains and our homes. We wanted our wives and children to be proud of us, after we were killed.

Roman cities and towns are all very fine, but you get no sense of belonging there. I'd rather live on a farm that my ancestors have worked for centuries. Our farmhouse is very snug, and we can mend it ourselves! We don't have to rely on expensive stone-masons and carpenters. Our clothes may be a bit rough, but they are bright and comfortable.Our craftworkers make beautiful jewellery, too.

And what's the use of reading or writing? We Celts all have excellent memories. I can tell you many ancient stories, and the **druids** know all the history of our **tribe**. We're proud to be Celts!"

A Celtic warrior

A Celtic farm

Why did the Romans

The Romans finally left Britain because, first and foremost, the Roman **empire** had grown so big that it was impossible to defend it all.

Roman emperors

There were also problems in Rome. The **emperors** were often weak, cruel or foolish. They quarrelled with everyone and spent years fighting wars at home.

Rebels in Britain

There were problems in Britain, as well. Many rich Romans there were lazy, living comfortably in their towns and villas instead of helping the soldiers to guard the **frontiers**. Some Roman governors supported Celtic peoples in Britain who wanted to end Roman rule, others rebelled against the emperors in Rome.

Invaders attack

Around AD 370 the Roman empire was attacked by many different invaders. Picts and Scots came from Scotland and Ireland. Saxons came from Germany. They attacked Britain. Vandals and Visigoths came from north-east Europe. Huns came from Asia. They kept on attacking the city of Rome. Each time they attacked, the emperor called soldiers back from distant lands like Britain to help fight against the new enemy.

The Romans leave

In AD 406, enemy tribes invaded Gaul (France). The Roman army in Britain rushed there, hoping to drive them away. People in Britain wanted the Romans to come back and protect them, but in AD 410, the emperor in Rome announced that Britain would have to defend itself, and rule itself, from now on.

The Vandals conquering Rome, imagined by a 19th-century artist.

leave Britain?

Parts of Hadrian's Wall still stand today. But many stones have been taken away to use for local buildings.

Arrows on the map show how invaders attacked the Roman empire from all sides.

Glossary

aqueduct A bridge built to carry a water channel.

bard A Celtic poet and musician.

barracks Buildings where soldiers live.

betray To give away a secret which harms someone else.

citizens People who belong to a particular city or country.

comrades People who live and work together.

druid A Celtic priest.

emperor The ruler of an empire.

empire A group of countries controlled by one person or government.

engineers People who design and build machines, roads and bridges.

frontier The boundary between two countries.

government The group of people who organize the running of a country.

groma Tool used by Roman **engineers** to measure angles and make sure roads were built straight.

heroine A very brave girl or woman.

lawyer A person who knows all about the laws (rules) that everyone in a country must obey.

mosaic A pattern or picture made from tiny pieces of stone or glass, often found on a floor.

multi-cultural Made up of people from many cultures who have different customs and traditions.

politician A person who takes part in the government of a country

profession A responsible job that a person has to be trained for, such as teacher, doctor or soldier.

republic A country where the leader is chosen by the people who live there.

revenge To get your revenge means to harm someone who has harmed you.

taxes Money that people have to pay to the **government** to pay for important things like roads or the army.

torc A metal ring worn round the throat, for magic protection, or as jewellery.

traitor Someone who **betrays** his friends or country by giving away their secrets.

tribe A group of families living together in one area, ruled by a chief.

volunteers People who choose to do something, such as joining the army, without being forced.

Bibliography

Books

Connolly, P. *The Roman Fort*
ISBN 019 910462 3

Conolly, P. *The Legionary*
ISBN 019 910425 5

Conolly, P. *The Cavalryman*
ISBN 019 910424 7

James, S. *Ancient Rome*
ISBN 0 8631 8445 6

Macdonald, F. *A Roman Fort*
ISBN 0 7500 2283 3

Macdonald, F. *Romans and Celts*
ISBN 0 7500 1099 1

Macdonald, F. *Step into the Celtic World*
ISBN 0 7548 0215 9

Malam, J. *The Traveller's Guide to Ancient Rome*
ISBN 184028 051 4

Morley, J. *A Roman Villa*
ISBN 0 7500 2188 8

Steele, P. *Step into the Roman Empire*
ISBN 1 85967 526 3

Websites

Museums and sites:

London: www.museumoflondon.org.uk
www.thebritishmuseum.ac.uk/childrenscompass

Cardiff: www.nmgw.ac.uk/hmgc

Edinburgh: www.nms.ac.uk

Glasgow:
www.hunterian.gla.ac.uk/museum/museum_index.html

Bath: www.romanbaths.co.uk

Hadrian's Wall: www.hadrians-wall.org

Vindolanda (fort) www.vindolanda.com

Fishbourne (villa) www.sussexpast.co.uk

York www.york.gov.uk

Websites about Romans and Celts

www.english-heritage.org.uk

www.romans-in-britain.org.uk

www.bbc.co.uk/schools/romans

www.bbc.co.uk/scotland/education/seeyouseeme

www.historyforkids.org/learn/romans/index.htm

www.ketting.gov.uk/leisure/cultural/museum/romansandcelts/home.htm

Index